THE BIG HURT'S

GUIDE TO BBQ AND GRILLING

FRANK THOMAS

TRIUMPH
BOOKS

This book is available in quantity at special discounts for your group or organization. For further information, contact:

Triumph Books LLC
814 N. Franklin
Chicago, Illinois 60610
www.triumphbooks.com

Printed in United States of America
ISBN: 978-1-62937-229-7
Design by Andy Hansen
Page production by Patricia Frey
Cover and select photography by Paul Petrowsky
Photos on pages 8 and 30 courtesy of Newscom. Photos on pages 48, 70, 90, and 130 courtesy of AP Images.
Contributors: Adam Motin, Andrea Baird, Jesse Jordan, Lindsay Philiben, and Michelle Bruton

CONTENTS

INTRODUCTION

For as long as I can remember, food has been a huge part of my life. And now, with my playing days behind me, food has become my passion.

As I look back on my career, I realize just how many of my tastes have changed. My very understanding of food has evolved. With this book, I hope to take the wonderful dishes that I have grown to love—those grilling recipes that make summer amazing—and share them with you.

I grew up in the South, where eating is everything. At the center of that eating experience was the cookout. My dad loved it—he even made his own tub for grilling. And we'd be out there three, four days every week. Ribs and barbecue chicken every weekend. All my dad wanted was to get that grill smoking and have himself a day.

One of the dirty little secrets about growing up in the South though, with our love of hearty food and big portions: it's not exactly the healthiest way to live. The only vegetables we ate were corn and black-eyed peas. Which, at the time, was fine with me. Who likes vegetables as a kid? But at some point we all learn that you can't eat like that forever.

As I've gotten older I've learned so much more about eating well and making sure that the food I eat is the right kind of fuel. Today, I like my diet to be full of lean chicken and fish, of fruits and vegetables and interesting combinations that a kid from Georgia never would have imagined. Asparagus, broccoli, spinach—I love my greens. And now, I want to share this love with you.

Learning to find balance in your diet is vital. I'm a big Southern boy. I had to learn what foods were best for my body and how to better determine healthier portion sizes. You shouldn't eat in order to be full—you should eat to enjoy the food and feel good about yourself when you're done. With the right-sized helping of nutritious food, you can eat a perfectly healthy meal and still enjoy it.

I owe much of my love for and knowledge of food to baseball. Baseball really is a beautiful thing. It let me travel the country, meet different kinds of people, and try unique types of food as I encountered new cultures. Take sushi, for example. I hardly even knew sushi existed as a child, but now I eat it all the time! And it wasn't until the season I played in Oakland, where a great sushi scene exists, that I grew to truly love

it. I consider myself lucky to have traveled and experienced so much, to have grown up in Georgia and spent so much of my life in Chicago. With each place I've been, I've taken a bit of the culture and food with me. That's what I want to share with you in this book.

I created *The Big Hurt's Guide to BBQ and Grilling* for the same reason that I opened the Big Hurt Brewhouse in Berwyn, just outside of Chicago: I want to share my passion. I've learned how to enjoy these foods in a healthy way that keeps me cooking them up time and time again.

And, sure, I've still got plenty of the old-fashioned comfort food that every cookout needs. I want these fantastic recipes, ones that I've fallen in love with throughout the years, to reach as many people as possible. Whether it's a slab of ribs from the South, a juicy New York steak, or a refreshing California-style appetizer, I love them all. I hope you will, too.

35 HOF
2014

GRILLING BASICS

You can write an entire book on the basics of grilling—in fact, you might have one sitting on your bookshelf right now. Rather than going over what "BBQ" means in the South versus what it means up north, or describing the differences between a gas grill and a charcoal grill, I'm going to assume if you're reading this that you're at least familiar with the basic concept of cooking and grilling outdoors.

Here is a brief overview of some of the terms, guidelines, ingredients, and equipment discussed in this book.

ESSENTIAL INGREDIENTS

Brown sugar

Balsamic vinegar

Cayenne pepper

Chili powder

Red chili flakes

Apple cider vinegar

Ketchup

Paprika

All-purpose flour

Worcestershire sauce

Vegetable oil

Olive oil

Kosher and sea salts

Black pepper

ESSENTIAL TOOLS

Heat-resistant silicone gloves

Long-handled tongs

Long-handled spatula

Basting brush

Paper towels

Perforated grill pan

Meat thermometer

Digital timer

Resealable plastic bags

Disposable foil drip pans

Wood chunks

Aluminum foil

GRILLING TERMS

Whether you prefer the convenience and control of a gas grill or the heat potential of a charcoal kettle, the basic principles of grilling remain the same. Grilling over direct heat means just that—placing the food directly over the heat source. Larger pieces of meat are often cooked using indirect heat, wherein the fire or hot charcoal is contained on one side of the grill, while the food is placed on the opposite side, over the unlit portion.

SAFETY TIPS

Whether you're using a gas or charcoal grill, make sure you have read the manufacturer's instructions, that your grill is outdoors in a well-ventilated area, that your grill is stable atop a solid base, and that you never leave a grill unattended.

GRILLING TEMPERATURES

Every grill is different, but here are some basic rules of thumb for the recipes in this book.

High	450-600 degrees
Medium-high	400 degrees
Medium	325-350 degrees
Medium-low	300 degrees
Low	225-250 degrees

MINIMUM COOKING TEMPERATURES

Ground beef	160 degrees
Steaks	160 degrees
Beef roasts	145 degrees
Poultry	165 degrees

1

APPETIZERS

GRAND SLAM GRILLED GRAPES

Putting grapes on your grill may sound unusual, but trust me—fresh grapes, balsamic vinegar, and a good char make for a great combination. Serve with bread and cheese for a unique appetizer. For an added kick, add some red chili flakes.

SERVES 6

1 pound red seedless grapes, washed
½ cup extra virgin olive oil
3 tablespoons balsamic vinegar

2 garlic cloves, minced
1 container burrata or goat cheese
1 loaf Italian bread or baguette, sliced

1. Preheat grill to high.
2. Whisk the olive oil, balsamic vinegar, and garlic together in a large bowl, then add grapes and toss to evenly coat. It's easier to leave the grapes in one or two large bunches at this point.
3. When your grill is hot, place the grapes over direct heat for 30–45 seconds on each side.
4. Once the grapes are cool enough to handle, cut them into smaller bunches.
5. Brush the bread slices with olive oil, then toast on your grill and serve with the cheese of your choice.

GRILLED AVOCADOS WITH TOMATO AND CHEESE

Avocados offer almost 20 vitamins and minerals in every serving, and are low in sugar and high in fiber. They also contain a good amount of monounsaturated fat, aka the "good" kind of fat. Topping a grilled avocado with grilled tomato and a sprinkling of cheese makes this appetizer both nutritious and delicious.

SERVES 6

3 ripe avocados
3 small ripe tomatoes
1 tablespoon olive oil

3 tablespoons feta or goat cheese
Sea salt and ground black pepper, to taste

1. Preheat grill to medium-high.
2. Cut avocados in half and remove the seeds, then slice tomatoes in half. Brush all halves with olive oil.
3. Grill tomatoes cut side down over direct heat until they begin to char, about 2 minutes. Set aside to cool.
4. Grill avocados cut side down until grill marks begin to appear, about 2–3 minutes.
5. When cool enough to handle, dice the tomatoes and mix them in a small bowl with the cheese of your choice.
6. Top each avocado half with a generous spoonful of the tomato mixture, then season with sea salt and black pepper.

GRILLED PIZZA WITH PROSCIUTTO AND ARUGULA

I love turning my grill into a backyard pizza oven—I can reach temperatures that are impossible in a standard oven, which better mimics a true pizza oven, plus it avoids heating up my kitchen during hot Chicago summers. The dough in this recipe is almost foolproof and yields 2 small pizzas, perfect as a shared appetizer. Make sure you have all of your toppings at the ready once the dough is on the grill.

SERVES 6

¾ cup warm water

1 teaspoon active-dry or instant yeast

2 cups unbleached all-purpose flour

1½ teaspoons salt

⅔ cup tomato sauce

8 ounces mozzarella cheese, evenly sliced

1 cup arugula

6 ounces prosciutto, thinly sliced

GRILLED PIZZA WITH PROSCIUTTO AND ARUGULA
(continued)

1. Pour the water and yeast into a small bowl. Stir until the yeast has dissolved and the mixture resembles thin soup, then pour it into a large mixing bowl with the flour and salt and mix until you've formed a shaggy dough. Transfer the dough to a lightly floured work surface—I like to use a marble pastry board. Knead until the dough is smooth and elastic, about 5 minutes, then place in a lightly oiled bowl and cover with plastic wrap or a kitchen towel for 90 minutes.

2. Preheat grill to high, preferably to at least 500 degrees. If you have a pizza stone, put it in the middle of your grill and allow it to heat for at least 30 minutes. (You can also use a standard sheet pan.)

3. Tear off 2 pieces of parchment paper roughly 12 inches wide. Divide the dough in half and use the heel of your hand to stretch each half on a piece of parchment paper until it's about ¼-inch thick—don't worry if they're not perfect circles.

4. Spoon half the sauce into the center of each pizza and spread it out to the edges, then top each pizza with cheese. Slide the first pizza, including parchment paper, onto your pizza stone or sheet pan, and allow to cook until the dough releases from the parchment paper, about 5 minutes. Carefully slide out the parchment paper, then continue to cook the pizza until the cheese begins to bubble and brown, about 3-5 minutes. Top with half of the prosciutto and arugula. Repeat the process for the second pizza.

5. Let each pizza cool for about 5 minutes before serving.

GRILLED OYSTERS WITH CHORIZO

Don't be afraid of grilling oysters! They're easier to cook than you think, and topping them with spicy chorizo and butter makes for a mouthwatering appetizer. Try to find larger oysters—they're less likely to dry out.

SERVES 6

6 ounces fresh Mexican chorizo, casing removed
1½ sticks unsalted butter, cut into small cubes

2 tablespoons lime juice
Salt, to taste
18 large oysters, scrubbed

1. Preheat grill to high.
2. Cook the chorizo in a cast-iron skillet, breaking it up with a spoon until the meat has browned, about 8 minutes. Transfer to a bowl and set aside to cool.
3. Add a tablespoon of water to the skillet and simmer, then add a few cubes of butter at a time, whisking constantly, until melted. Add the crumbled chorizo and lime juice and season with salt, then set aside.
4. Place the oysters on the grill over direct heat, flat side up, and close the lid. Cook until the shells open slightly, about 2 minutes. Transfer to a platter and carefully remove the top shell using a small knife or a screwdriver. Spoon the chorizo and butter mixture onto the oysters and serve immediately.

GRILLED VEGGIE-STUFFED PORTOBELLO

When I was a kid, we didn't see nearly enough vegetables, but now I can't get enough of them. This is a great meatless centerpiece for a healthy summer night of grilling.

SERVES 4

3 tablespoons balsamic vinegar
¼ cup extra virgin olive oil
2 teaspoons fresh thyme, chopped
2 teaspoons cilantro, chopped
¼ cup lemon juice
Zest of half a lemon
½ teaspoon salt
½ teaspoon ground black pepper

4 portobello mushrooms, stemmed, gills cut out and discarded
1 zucchini, sliced lengthwise into ½-inch thick strips
1 red or orange bell pepper, halved and seeded
1 yellow bell pepper, halved and seeded
½ red onion, halved
Salt and ground black pepper, to taste

1. Whisk balsamic vinegar, olive oil, thyme, cilantro, lemon juice, lemon zest, and salt and pepper in a large bowl.
2. Preheat grill to medium-high.
3. Add the portobello mushrooms, zucchini, peppers, and onion to the bowl with the dressing and toss to coat.
4. When your grill is hot, cook the mushrooms, zucchini, peppers, and onion over direct heat until grill marks begin to appear, about 6-8 minutes per side.
5. When zucchini, peppers, and onions are cool enough to handle, dice them into bite-size pieces and toss them back into the dressing. Plate portobello mushroom caps upside down and fill them with the diced vegetables, then add salt and black pepper to taste.

TOMATO AND HERB FRITTATA

Baking in your grill with a cast-iron skillet is a great alternative to using your oven, especially during long, hot summers. This satisfying egg dish is easy to make and uses ingredients you probably already have in your kitchen.

SERVES 6

5-7 large eggs
1 teaspoon salt
½ teaspoon ground black pepper
½ onion, diced
1 green bell pepper, diced
2 garlic cloves, minced

1 cup fresh spinach, chopped
1 14.5-ounce can diced tomatoes, drained
¼ cup fresh herbs, such as parsley, thyme, or chives
½ tomato, sliced
¾ cup Parmesan cheese

1. Preheat grill to high.
2. Beat eggs, salt, and black pepper in a large bowl and set aside.
3. Grease the bottom and sides of the cast-iron skillet with vegetable oil, then place on the grill to warm. When the pan is hot, saute onion and green pepper over direct heat until they begin to soften, about 5 minutes.
4. Add garlic, spinach, and diced tomatoes to the pan and saute for another 2-3 minutes.
5. Pour the eggs into the pan and stir to evenly combine all the ingredients. Place sliced tomatoes across the top and sprinkle entire pan with cheese.
6. Move the pan over indirect heat and close the lid. Bake for about 15-20 minutes, or until the frittata has set and the top is slightly browned. Allow the frittata to cool, in the skillet, for 5 minutes before slicing.

BRUSCHETTA WITH GRILLED BELL PEPPERS, ZUCCHINI, OLIVES, AND MOZZARELLA

Bruschetta is a fool-proof appetizer for when you're hosting a group of people. Grilled peppers and zucchini brings in the feel of summer.

SERVES 8

1 zucchini, sliced
1 red bell pepper, quartered
1 orange bell pepper, quartered
1 tablespoon olive oil
1 loaf Italian bread or baguette, sliced

6 black olives, sliced
4 ounces fresh mozzarella cheese, thinly sliced
¾ cup basil
Salt and ground black pepper, to taste

1. Preheat grill to medium.
2. Add the zucchini, bell peppers, and olive oil to a large bowl and toss to evenly coat.
3. When your grill is hot, transfer the vegetables to a perforated grill pan over direct heat and cook, turning occasionally, until nicely charred, about 3-5 minutes. When the peppers are cool enough to handle, slice each quarter in half.
4. Brush the bread slices with olive oil, then toast on your grill. Transfer the bread to a large platter and top each slice with zucchini, peppers, olives, mozzarella, and basil. Add salt and black pepper to taste.

SPICED AND SMOKY NUTS

Baseball and peanuts go hand in hand, but this is a great way to add some flavor and variety to what can be an ordinary snack. You can use a mix of almonds, pecans, cashews, or any other nuts you enjoy.

SERVES 6

1 teaspoon brown sugar
1 teaspoon dried thyme
¼ teaspoon ground cayenne pepper

¼ teaspoon mustard powder
2 cups salted nuts
2 teaspoons extra virgin olive oil

1. Soak 3-4 cups of wood chunks in cold water for 45-60 minutes and then drain.
2. Preheat grill to medium.
3. Mix the brown sugar, thyme, cayenne pepper, and mustard powder in a small bowl.
4. Pour the nuts into a disposable foil roasting pan, then drizzle with olive oil. Add the seasoning mixture and toss to coat evenly, spreading the nuts out in a single layer.
5. Transfer the wood chips to a smoker box or vented foil pouch and heat until they begin to smoke. Place the pan of nuts on the indirect side of the grill and close the lid. Cook until the nuts are toasted, about 20-30 minutes, stirring the nuts every so often to avoid burning.
6. Let the nuts cool in the pan before serving.

CHEESY GRILLED MUSSELS

Mussels make for a great appetizer when there's a crowd around. You can get them cleaned and debearded at any good seafood counter.

SERVES 6–8

¼ cup unsalted butter, softened
¼ cup Parmesan cheese, finely grated
2 garlic cloves, minced
½ onion, shredded

24 mussels, scrubbed and debearded
Kosher salt and ground black pepper, to taste

1. Preheat grill to medium.
2. Add the butter, cheese, garlic, and onions to a bowl, then mix to combine.
3. When your grill is hot, cook the mussels over direct heat, with the lid closed, until their shells open, about 3-5 minutes. Transfer them to a platter, discarding any mussels that did not open. Place a cast-iron pan on the grill and close the lid.
4. When the mussels are cool enough to handle, crack off the top shell and spoon some of the cheese mixture over each. Carefully place the mussels shell side down in the cast-iron pan, in batches if necessary, and cook with the lid closed until the cheese is bubbling, about 3-5 minutes. Season with salt and black pepper.

2

SIDES

GRILLED ASPARAGUS WITH PARMESAN AND SEA SALT

Grilling asparagus brings out the vegetable's natural flavor, is easy to do, and makes for a versatile side dish. It works equally well with chicken and steaks as it does with a hearty piece of salmon or tuna.

SERVES 4

1 pound asparagus
2 tablespoons extra virgin olive oil
Ground black pepper, to taste

½ cup Parmesan cheese, thinly sliced or grated
Sea salt, to taste

1. Preheat grill to high.
2. Slice off the bottom 2 inches of the asparagus spears, then toss them in a bowl with the olive oil and black pepper until evenly coated.
3. When your grill is hot, place the asparagus spears diagonally across the grill grates. Cook over direct heat, turning frequently, until all sides are nicely charred, about 8-10 minutes. Increase or decrease the cooking time, depending on how firm you prefer your asparagus.
4. Place the asparagus on a large plate and sprinkle with the cheese and sea salt.

GRILLED POTATO SALAD

This is a simple and light potato salad that makes a perfect side for a lot of different meals. Grilling the potatoes gives them a great flavor and keeps them from getting soft, and the mustard-garlic mixture packs a wallop.

SERVES 4

2 pounds small yellow potatoes, quartered or halved

Kosher salt, to taste

2 tablespoons fresh oregano, minced

2 tablespoons fresh parsley leaves, minced

4 garlic cloves, minced

¼ cup extra virgin olive oil

Ground black pepper, to taste

1 tablespoon whole grain mustard

2 tablespoons vegetable oil

8 pearl onions, halved

1 pint cherry tomatoes

1 whole lemon, halved

3 sprigs fresh rosemary

GRILLED POTATO SALAD
(continued)

1. Place potatoes in a large pot and cover with cold water. Season generously with salt and bring to a boil on your stove over high heat. Simmer until potatoes are tender, about 5 minutes, then drain them and allow to cool.

2. When potatoes are cool enough to handle, slice into quarters or halves, depending on size, and place them in a large bowl. Add half of oregano, half of parsley, half of garlic, and half of olive oil. Season to taste with salt and black pepper and toss until potatoes are evenly coated. Combine remaining oregano, parsley, garlic, olive oil, and mustard in a large bowl.

3. Preheat grill to medium-high. When your grill is hot, use tongs to dip a wad of paper towels in vegetable oil and run them a dozen times across the grates. Cook potatoes over direct heat, turning occasionally, until brown and crispy on both sides, about 5-8 minutes. Transfer potatoes to the bowl with the olive oil and herb mixture as they finish cooking.

4. In a bowl, toss onions and tomatoes with vegetable oil, then place them on a perforated grill pan over direct heat, turning occasionally, until nicely charred, about 5 minutes.

5. Place lemon halves cut side down and grill until browned, about 5 minutes. Squeeze one half into bowl with potatoes and toss to coat evenly. Season to taste with salt and black pepper, then pull and shred the rosemary sprigs and sprinkle over top. Use other lemon half as a garnish.

GRILLED TOMATO GAZPACHO

A nice, refreshing gazpacho makes a great side dish in the summertime, especially if your main dish is on the heavier side. Grilling the tomatoes gives this soup a deep, smoky flavor.

SERVES 6

2 garlic cloves, unpeeled
3 pounds plum tomatoes
½ small red onion, peeled and halved
1 jalapeño pepper
1 slice sourdough or country bread
1 cucumber, peeled and sliced

1 cup tomato juice
1 tablespoon sherry vinegar
½ teaspoon Kosher salt
¼ cup extra virgin olive oil
½ cup diced cucumber

1. Preheat grill to medium.
2. When your grill is hot, place the garlic, plum tomatoes, onion, and jalapeño pepper over direct heat and close the lid. Turn them occasionally, until they are softened and grill marks begin to show, about 8-15 minutes. Transfer the vegetables to a baking sheet.
3. When they are cool enough to handle, peel and core the tomatoes and then cut them into chunks—do this over the baking sheet to catch all the juices. Peel the garlic, chop the onion, peel and deseed the jalapeño, and tear the bread into pieces.
4. Combine the tomatoes, garlic, onion, jalapeño, torn bread, cucumber slices, tomato juice, vinegar, salt, olive oil, and any collected juices from the baking sheet in your blender or food processor and blend until well pureed, about 1-2 minutes. Pour the gazpacho into an airtight container and refrigerate until cold.
5. To serve, pour the gazpacho into bowls and garnish with diced cucumber.

GRILLED SWEET POTATOES

Most people think of sweet potatoes as a Thanksgiving dish, but grilling them makes them crunchy and charred on the outside, sweet and creamy on the inside. You can follow the recipe below to simply cook the potatoes or do what I do—mix together some chopped cilantro, lime, and cayenne for some added spice.

SERVES 4

3-4 medium-sized sweet potatoes
3 tablespoons olive oil
1 tablespoon Kosher salt

¼ cup cilantro, minced
1 teaspoon cayenne pepper
Zest of half a lime

1. Poke about a dozen holes in each sweet potato. Line a microwave-safe dish with paper towels, then place two potatoes on the plate and set the microwave on high for 4-5 minutes. Carefully turn the potatoes over and cook for another 4-5 minutes. Do the same with the other two potatoes. When cool enough to handle, cut the potatoes into half and then into wedges (or, simply cut them into 1-inch circular slices).

2. Preheat grill to high.

3. Brush the potatoes with oil and season with salt and pepper. When your grill is hot, cook the potatoes until slightly charred, about 2-3 minutes per side.

4. In a small bowl, mix salt, cilantro, cayenne pepper, and lime zest, then sprinkle over the potatoes.

MEXICAN STREET CORN

Chicago has a large and vibrant Hispanic community, and over the years I came to love a lot of Mexican cuisine. This recipe for elotes takes regular corn on the cob and turns it into a tangy, spicy, and messy side dish.

SERVES 4

4 ears shucked corn
½ cup Mexican crema, or sour cream
    diluted with a little milk
⅓ cup queso fresco, or Parmesan cheese

1 tablespoon chili powder
¼ cup cilantro, minced
1 lime, quartered

1. Preheat grill to high.
2. In a large bowl, mix the crema or sour cream, most but not all of the cheese, chili powder, and cilantro. Set aside.
3. When your grill is hot, place the corn over direct heat and cook, turning frequently, until all sides are slightly charred, about 8-10 minutes.
4. Place the hot corn into the bowl and slather with the crema mixture. Serve immediately with the remaining cheese for sprinkling and limes for squeezing.

SKILLET MAC AND CHEESE

Macaroni and cheese cooked in a cast-iron pan makes for a rich, indulgent side to any grilled dish. This recipe includes cayenne pepper to give the pasta a kick. Now isn't the time to cut down on butter or use skim milk; the higher the fat content in the dish, the creamier the final result will be.

SERVES 4

One 12-ounce box elbow macaroni
1 teaspoon olive oil
1 tablespoon butter
1½ cups whole milk
1 teaspoon dry mustard
½ teaspoon paprika

½ teaspoon cayenne pepper
½ teaspoon salt
2½ cups grated cheese of your choice (try a mix of cheddar, gouda, and havarti)
4-5 tablespoons all-purpose flour
1 teaspoon parsley, chopped

1. Bring a large pot of salted water to a boil on your stovetop, then add the macaroni and cook until al dente. Pour the cooked pasta into a strainer and toss with olive oil to prevent from sticking.
2. Grease the bottom and sides of the cast-iron skillet with vegetable oil, then place on the grill to warm. When the pan is hot, melt the butter, then add the milk, mustard, paprika, cayenne pepper, and salt, and stir to combine.
3. Whisk the grated cheese into the skillet mixture one handful at a time, reserving ½ cup of cheese. When the cheese is melted, sift flour over the skillet, one tablespoon at a time, whisking constantly, until the sauce thickens.
4. Add the cooked pasta to the skillet and fold until combined. Sprinkle the top of the mixture with the reserved grated cheese.
5. Cover the grill and cook until the top of the macaroni is browned and bubbly, about 5 minutes. Sprinkle with parsley and serve.

FOIL POUCH GREEN BEANS AND ONIONS

Grilling in foil is quick, easy, and involves minimal clean-up. These green beans and onions get steamed and caramelized at the same time, and the minced garlic gives them a kick. Top with a pat of butter and a sprinkle of red chili flakes for extra flavor.

SERVES 4

1 pound green beans, ends trimmed
½ white onion, diced
½ teaspoon Kosher salt
½ teaspoon ground black pepper
4 garlic cloves, minced

1 tablespoon olive oil
1 tablespoon water
1 tablespoon butter
1 teaspoon red chili flakes
Juice of half a lemon

1. Lay two sheets of aluminum foil on top of one another, then place the beans and diced onion in the middle of the top sheet. Sprinkle salt, black pepper, and garlic over vegetables, then drizzle with olive oil and water. Fold the foil over lengthwise first, then fold in the ends. Be sure the packet is tightly sealed.

2. Preheat grill to medium.

3. When your grill is hot, place the foil packet over direct heat for 7 minutes with the lid closed. Flip the packet and cook for another 7 minutes.

4. Carefully open the packet and make sure beans and onions are tender before removing from grill. Empty vegetables onto a platter and top with butter, red chili flakes, and lemon juice.

"HOT" GRILLED BROCCOLI

I know what you're thinking—eating broccoli is like taking your medicine, something you've tried to avoid since you were a kid. But I love grilled broccoli as an adult, and trust me, once you've prepared it this way, it'll become a regular part of your summer menu.

SERVES 4

3-4 crowns fresh broccoli
3 tablespoons olive oil
½ tablespoon Worcestershire sauce
½ tablespoon hot sauce

½ tablespoon Kosher salt
½ tablespoon cracked black pepper
½ tablespoon garlic powder
1 teaspoon red chili flakes

1. Preheat grill to high.
2. Separate the stalks from the broccoli, then rinse the heads and drain thoroughly. Transfer them to a large container with a lid, then add the olive oil and shake until the broccoli is evenly coated. Remove the lid and add Worcestershire sauce, hot sauce, salt, black pepper, garlic powder, and red chili flakes, then reseal lid and shake again to mix all the ingredients.

3. Tear off a sheet of aluminum foil large enough to fit the broccoli in a single layer, then lay the foil on the grill and quickly spread the broccoli out on it. Close the lid and cook until the broccoli is cooked but still firm, about 8-10 minutes. Carefully remove the entire sheet of foil from your grill—the broccoli should mostly slide right off.

3

BURGERS,
HOT DOGS
AND SAUSAGES

BEER-BRAISED BRATS WITH SAUERKRAUT

I'd never had a bratwurst until I came up to Chicago. But like everyone else, I fell in love. This is the way to go, too—bratwurst braised in your favorite beer with tangy sauerkraut and a good spicy brown mustard.

SERVES 4

24 ounces beer
2½ tablespoons brown sugar
4 bratwursts

3 cups refrigerated sauerkraut, rinsed and drained
½ teaspoon ground black pepper

1. Preheat grill to medium.
2. Mix the beer and brown sugar in a disposable aluminum pan, then place over direct heat and bring to a simmer. Add the sauerkraut and bratwurst to the pan, close the lid, and turn the heat down to medium-low—you want to braise the bratwursts at a soft simmer, not a boil.
3. Remove the bratwursts after 15-20 minutes and raise the heat to medium-high. Grill the bratwursts over direct heat, turning frequently, until the internal temperature reaches 160 degrees, about 6-8 minutes. Cook the remaining sauerkraut, uncovered, stirring frequently, as the liquid continues to reduce, about 5-10 minutes. Season with black pepper.
4. Place each cooked bratwurst into a bratwurst or hot dog bun and top with sauerkraut and spicy brown mustard.

BISON BURGER

Bison is a great alternative to ground beef—it's lower in saturated fat and has fewer calories despite packing a similar amount of protein. It can, however, get a little dry, which is why I like to add a little cheddar cheese and butter to each burger.

SERVES 4

2 pounds ground bison
¼ cup cheddar cheese
1 tablespoon Kosher salt

2 teaspoons ground black pepper
4 pats unsalted butter

1. Preheat grill to high.
2. Place the cheddar cheese and butter in your freezer until they begin to harden, about 4-5 minutes. Mix cheese, bison, salt, and black pepper in a large bowl until just combined, being careful not to overmix. Divide into four equal segments and form each segment into a patty, pressing your thumb into the center of each burger to form an indentation. Place a pat of butter inside each.

3. When your grill is hot, use tongs to dip a wad of paper towels in vegetable oil and run them a dozen times across the grates. Grill each burger over direct heat with the lid closed until cooked to medium, about 4-5 minutes per side. If desired, top burgers with any remaining cheese in the last 3 minutes.
4. Place each burger on a hearty bun and top with your favorite condiments.

CHICAGO-STYLE ALL-BEEF CHAR DOG

Grilling hot dogs might seem self-explanatory, but I'd be remiss if I didn't include a recipe directly from my adopted hometown. Three crucial elements to a Chicago hot dog? Poppy-seed buns, celery salt, and all-beef franks. Whether you put ketchup on yours should remain between you and your conscience!

SERVES 6

6 100% all-beef hot dogs
24 ounces beer
6 poppy-seed hot dog buns
6 tablespoons yellow mustard
1 medium onion, chopped

6 tablespoons sweet pickle relish
6 pickle spears
12 sport peppers, or pepperoncini
Celery salt, to taste
1 tomato, sliced and then halved

1. Preheat grill to high.
2. Pour beer into a disposable aluminum pan, then add the hot dogs. When your grill is hot, place the pan over direct heat until the beer begins to simmer, about 7-8 minutes. Move the pan to the cooler side of your grill, close the lid, and allow the hot dogs to completely cook through, about 10 minutes.
3. Remove hot dogs from the beer and cook over direct heat until grill marks begin to appear, turning frequently, about 2-3 minutes.
4. Place each hot dog in a poppy-seed bun and top with mustard, onions, pickle relish, pickles, peppers, celery salt, and tomatoes.

FRIED EGG BACON BURGER

I love a good burger, though I don't eat them as often as I used to. That's why I go all out when I do decide to treat myself, and adding bacon and a fried egg on top makes this one a decadent indulgence. And don't toss out those bacon drippings!

SERVES 4

8 bacon strips
1-2 slices white bread, crusts removed, cut into ½-inch pieces
¼ cup milk
1½ pounds ground beef (85-90% lean)

1 teaspoon salt
½ teaspoon ground black pepper
1 garlic clove, minced
2 tablespoons olive oil
4 eggs

1. Preheat grill to high.
2. In a large cast-iron skillet, fry bacon until crisp, about 8 minutes. Drain on paper towels. Spoon all of the bacon fat into a small bowl and refrigerate until cool.
3. Place bread and milk in a small bowl and allow them to soak for 5 minutes, then mash with fork to form a paste. Place ground beef, salt, black pepper, garlic, bread paste, and cooled bacon fat in a large bowl and mix until just combined, being careful not to overmix. Divide into four equal segments and form each segment into a patty, pressing your thumb into the center of each burger to form an indentation.
4. When your grill is hot, use tongs to dip a wad of paper towels in vegetable oil and run them a dozen times across the grates. Grill each burger, indentation side up, over direct heat with the lid closed for about 5 minutes. Flip and cook for 3-4 minutes on the other side, then set aside and cover with aluminum foil.
5. Heat the olive oil in your cast-iron skillet over medium-high heat, then fry each egg until the yolks are set but still runny, about 5 minutes.
6. Place each burger on a hearty bun and top with bacon, egg, and your favorite condiments.

SIRLOIN-AND-BRISKET BURGER WITH ROQUEFORT CHEESE AND CARAMELIZED ONIONS

This recipe was inspired by a burger I had once in New York—the mix of meats makes for a deliciously beefy flavor, and while I know bleu cheeses aren't for everyone, trust me, Roquefort cheese atop one of these burgers is awesome.

SERVES 4

2 tablespoons unsalted butter

2 yellow onions, thinly sliced

10 ounces boneless short rib

10 ounces beef brisket

12 ounces chuck roast

Kosher salt and ground black pepper, to taste

8 ounces Roquefort cheese

SIRLOIN-AND-BRISKET BURGER WITH ROQUEFORT CHEESE AND CARAMELIZED ONIONS (continued)

1. Ask the butcher at your local supermarket to grind the short rib, beef brisket, and chuck roast for you. If that is not an option, cut all of the meat into 1-inch pieces and place them on a baking sheet, then put them into the freezer until the meat is firm but not frozen, about 15-20 minutes. Working in batches, grind the meat in a food processor until consistent, then transfer to a large bowl and refrigerate.

2. Preheat grill to medium-low. Melt the butter in a cast-iron pan, then add the onions and cook, stirring infrequently, until they are golden brown and caramelized, about 45 minutes. Season with salt and black pepper and set aside. Turn grill up to high.

3. Mix the ground meat until just combined, being careful not to overmix. Divide into four equal segments and form each segment into a patty, pressing your thumb into the center of each burger to form an indentation. Season all sides with salt and black pepper.

4. When your grill is hot, use tongs to dip a wad of paper towels in vegetable oil and run them a dozen times across the grates. Grill each burger, indentation side up, over direct heat with the lid closed for 2 minutes. Flip burgers and cook for 2 more minutes, then move to indirect heat until cooked to medium, about 3 minutes. Transfer burgers to a foil-lined plate, top each with 2 ounces Roquefort cheese, and cover with more foil for 5 minutes.

5. Place each burger on a hearty bun and top with some of the caramelized onions.

ROASTED POBLANO CHEESEBURGERS WITH AVOCADO

Poblanos are one of the most popular peppers in Mexican cooking, and their thick skins make them perfect for grilling. If you're worried about them being too spicy for you, don't—they're hotter than a green pepper but not as hot as a jalapeño. Pairing them with some Monterey Jack cheese and the richness of avocado makes for one tasty burger.

SERVES 4

2 poblano peppers
1½ pounds ground beef (85-90% lean)
1 teaspoon salt
½ teaspoon ground black pepper

1 garlic clove, minced
4 slices Monterey Jack cheese
1 large avocado, mashed
Kosher salt, to taste

1. Preheat grill to high.
2. When your grill is hot, roast the poblanos over direct heat until their skin is blackened on all sides, about 15 minutes. Wrap the peppers in a clean kitchen towel and allow them to cool—the longer you wait, the easier it is to remove the skin. Also discard the stem and seeds, then cut each pepper in half.
3. Place ground beef, salt, black pepper, and garlic in a large bowl and mix until just combined, being careful not to overmix. Divide into four equal segments and form each segment into a patty, pressing your thumb into the center of each burger to form an indentation.
4. Use tongs to dip a wad of paper towels in vegetable oil and run them a dozen times across the grates. Grill each burger, indentation side up, over direct heat with the lid closed for about 5 minutes. Flip and cook for 3-4 minutes on the other side. During the last minute, place a slice of cheese on each burger. Set the finished cheeseburgers aside and cover with aluminum foil.
5. Place each burger on a hearty bun and top with a piece of the poblano. Spread the avocado evenly on the other side of the buns and sprinkle with Kosher salt.

SOUTHERN STYLE BURGER WITH COLLARD GREENS AND GREEN TOMATOES

Here's a burger with a Southern twist—it features collard greens and green tomatoes instead of the traditional lettuce and red tomato. The greens, a staple of Southern cooking, add a peppery twist, and the green tomatoes provide a firm base for a chow-chow-style relish.

SERVES 4

1 bunch collard greens
4 tablespoons extra virgin olive oil
1 large red onion, diced
4 garlic cloves, minced
1 teaspoon celery seeds
1 teaspoon dill
1 tablespoon black mustard seeds
1 teaspoon turmeric
1 teaspoon cayenne pepper

2 green tomatoes, diced
2 tablespoons white vinegar
2 tablespoons sugar
½ cup water
1½ pounds ground beef (85-90 percent lean)
Salt and ground black pepper, to taste

1. Remove the stems from the collard greens and thinly slice the leaves. Place the leaves in a bowl and drizzle with 2 tablespoons of olive oil, then season with salt and black pepper.

2. Heat 2 tablespoons of olive oil in a large pot over medium-high heat. When the oil is hot, add the onion, garlic, celery seeds, dill, black mustard seeds, turmeric, and cayenne pepper. Cook, stirring frequently, until the vegetables have softened and the mustard seeds have started to pop, about 3-4 minutes. Transfer half the mixture to a large bowl and set aside to cool. Add the green tomato, vinegar, sugar, and water to the pot, and season with salt and black pepper. Cook, stirring occasionally, until the mixture has thickened, about 15 minutes.

3. Preheat grill to high.

4. Place ground beef and the cooled half of the vegetable mixture in a large bowl and mix until just combined, being careful not to overmix. Divide into four equal segments and form each segment into a patty, pressing your thumb into the center of each burger to form an indentation.

5. When your grill is hot, use tongs to dip a wad of paper towels in vegetable oil and run them a dozen times across the grates. Grill each burger, indentation side up, over direct heat with the lid closed for about 5 minutes. Flip and cook for 3-4 minutes on the other side, then set aside and cover with aluminum foil.

6. Place each burger on a hearty bun and top with some of the warm green tomatoes and a handful of collard greens.

ZESTY BLACK BEAN PUMPKIN BURGERS

Vegetarian grilling doesn't mean skimping on flavor. These black bean pumpkin burgers are thick and almost meaty in texture, and can be customized to your liking with spices. In this burger, we're adding some zest with grated lemon and some heat with red chili flakes.

SERVES 6

1 15-ounce can black beans, drained and rinsed
⅓ cup panko
3 garlic cloves, minced
½ cup pumpkin puree
1 teaspoon chili powder
1 teaspoon cumin
½ teaspoon Kosher salt

½ teaspoon ground black pepper
Zest of half a lemon
⅛ cup cilantro, chopped
⅛ teaspoon ground white pepper
½ teaspoon red chili flakes
12 spinach leaves
6 slices fresh mozzarella cheese
1 avocado, sliced

---

1. Be sure all excess moisture is squeezed out of black beans, then add them and the panko to your food processor, pulsing for 30 seconds to combine.

2. In a medium bowl, combine garlic, pumpkin puree, chili powder, cumin, salt, black pepper, lemon zest, cilantro, white pepper, and red chili flakes, then empty contents of food processor into bowl and mix thoroughly. Divide mixture in half, then form three patties out of each half, pressing your thumb into the center of each patty to form an indentation.

3. Preheat grill to medium heat. When your grill is hot, use tongs to dip a wad of paper towels in vegetable oil and run them a dozen times across the grates. Grill each burger, indentation side up first, over direct heat with the lid closed for about 5 minutes on each side.

4. Arrange patties on buns and top with spinach, mozzarella, and avocado.

SOUTHERN FAVORITES

BARBECUE CHICKEN WITH ALABAMA WHITE BBQ SAUCE

Most people think of barbecue sauce as red, but in Alabama, they have a long tradition of eating white barbecue sauce. Everyone in the South has their favorite version—some like it thin and spicy, others creamier and tangier. Either way, it's a classic sauce for barbecued chicken and a ton of other dishes.

SERVES 6

5-6 pounds of your favorite chicken parts (legs, thighs, wings, breasts), skin-on
2 cups cider vinegar
1 cup vegetable oil
1 tablespoon poultry seasoning
1 egg
Kosher salt and ground black pepper, to taste

Alabama White BBQ Sauce
1½ cups mayonnaise
¼ cup water
¼ cup white wine vinegar
1 tablespoon coarsely ground pepper
1 tablespoon Creole mustard
1 teaspoon salt
1 teaspoon sugar
1 teaspoon garlic powder
1 teaspoon cayenne pepper
2 teaspoons prepared horseradish

1. Mix cider vinegar, oil, poultry seasoning, and egg in a blender until smooth. Place the chicken thighs in a large resealable bag, then pour in the marinade and make sure the chicken is well covered. Refrigerate for 2 hours.

2. Preheat grill to medium-high. Remove the chicken from the bag and pat dry.

3. When your grill is hot, use tongs to dip a wad of paper towels in vegetable oil and run them a dozen times across the grates. Grill chicken over direct heat, turning as needed and basting often with the other half of the marinade, until slightly charred and cooked through, or until the internal temperature of a chicken thigh reads 165 degrees, about 20–30 minutes.

4. In a large bowl, whisk together the mayonnaise, water, vinegar, black pepper, mustard, salt, sugar, garlic powder, cayenne pepper, and horseradish until well combined. Drizzle some over the chicken pieces and serve the rest of the sauce on the side.

BUTTERED CAST-IRON CORNBREAD

Authentic Southern cornbread is not the sweetened version that I found when I came to Chicago. This recipe features a fluffy, unsweetened bread that makes a perfect side to any BBQ dish. If you prefer a thinner cornbread, use a 10-inch skillet. For a smoky flavor, grease the pan with bacon drippings. For a kick, add green hatch chiles to the batter.

SERVES 8

1 cup coarsely ground yellow cornmeal

2 teaspoons Kosher salt

1 tablespoon double-acting baking powder

1 cup buttermilk

8 tablespoons melted unsalted butter

2 large eggs, beaten

1. Preheat grill to medium heat. Grease the bottom and sides of the cast-iron skillet with vegetable oil, then place on the grill to warm.

2. In a large bowl, combine the cornmeal, salt, and baking powder. In another bowl, mix the buttermilk, butter, and eggs, then add them into the dry mixture and mix to combine.

3. Spread the batter evenly in the hot skillet and cook, uncovered, until the edges become crisp, about 5-10 minutes. Close the lid and cook until a toothpick inserted in the center comes out clean, about 20 minutes.

4. Allow the cornbread to cool, in the skillet, for 5 minutes to avoid crumbling. Place a pat of butter on each piece and serve warm.

CLASSIC BBQ BAKED BEANS

No cookout in the South is complete without baked beans. This is a simple recipe that combines sweet and smoky ingredients for a thick, rich, and perfect side dish.

SERVES 6

¼ pound thick-cut bacon, diced
½ large onion, chopped
1 red pepper, chopped
3 16-ounce cans kidney beans
½ cup brown sugar
3 tablespoons ketchup
3 tablespoons apple cider vinegar

3 tablespoons maple syrup
3 tablespoons molasses
3 tablespoons yellow mustard
1 tablespoon hot sauce
2 teaspoons Creole seasoning

1. Preheat grill to high.
2. Place a large Dutch oven or cast-iron pot over direct heat and cook bacon until fat has begun to render. Add onion and red pepper and cook until they begin to soften, about 3-5 minutes. Add the beans, including canning liquid, and bring to a simmer.
3. Add brown sugar, ketchup, apple cider vinegar, maple syrup, molasses, mustard, hot sauce, and Creole seasoning and stir to combine. Close the lid and cook the beans until the liquid has thickened, about 60 minutes. Cover the pot and move to the cooler side of the grill, then cook for another 20-30 minutes or until desired tenderness.

GRILLED GUMBO

Gumbo is serious business down South. It starts with a roux and the classic trinity of onion, pepper, and celery. You can spend all day making a gumbo, as my dad often did when I was a kid, but this simplified recipe is great for any Sunday afternoon. Grilling the vegetables, shrimp, and andouille sausage adds a ton of flavor. I highly recommend adding some filé powder, a classic Southern herb made from the ground leaves of the sassafras tree.

SERVES 4–6

2 tablespoons vegetable oil

1 large white onion, halved

2 large red or green bell peppers

6 garlic cloves, unpeeled

1 pound medium shrimp, peeled and
   deveined

Salt and ground black pepper, to taste

1 6-ounce smoked andouille sausage

4 tablespoons olive oil

4 tablespoons all-purpose flour

4 celery ribs, diced

1 tablespoon tomato paste

1 teaspoon paprika

¼ teaspoon cayenne pepper

1 14.5-ounce can of fire-roasted diced
   tomatoes

6 cups shrimp broth or chicken broth

2 cups okra, about 30-40 pods, chopped

1 tablespoon filé powder (optional)

GRILLED GUMBO (continued)

1. Preheat grill to high. When your grill is hot, use tongs to dip a wad of paper towels in vegetable oil and run them a dozen times across the grates. Grill the onion halves, pepper, and garlic over direct heat until nicely charred, turning frequently. When cool enough to handle, chop the onion halves and pepper, then peel the garlic cloves and mince them.

2. Meanwhile, season shrimp with salt and pepper, then grill for about 2 minutes per side or until nicely charred.

3. Over indirect heat, cook the sausage until heated through, about 8-10 minutes. Move the sausage over direct heat for 1-2 minutes more or until nicely charred. When cool enough to handle, slice sausage on the bias, at roughly a 45-degree angle.

4. In a large, heavy-bottomed soup pot, heat olive oil over medium-high on your stovetop. Sprinkle in flour and stir to combine. Continue cooking for about 5 minutes, stirring, until flour is well browned. Add celery, tomato paste, paprika, and cayenne pepper. Cook until celery has softened, stirring well, then add tomatoes and andouille sausage. Season mixture generously with salt and pepper.

5. Stir in broth and reduce heat to medium. With a wooden spoon, scrape bottom of pot to dissolve any browned bits. Simmer for 25-30 minutes, until gumbo base thickens. Taste and season with salt, if necessary.

6. Add shrimp and okra and cook until the okra has softened, about 5 minutes. Stir in filé powder, if desired, and serve immediately.

GRILLED OKRA WITH CHIPOTLE SAUCE

I grew up eating okra, but I know it's not for everyone. Grilling okra over high heat, however, gives them a great texture, and the chipotle sauce will win over even the harshest critic. You can find canned chipotles in adobe sauce in almost any grocery store.

SERVES 6

1 pound okra
1 tablespoon olive oil
Kosher salt and ground black pepper, to taste
½ cup sour cream

¼ cup mayonnaise
1 chipotle in adobo, roughly chopped
1 tablespoon adobo sauce
1 tablespoon lime juice

1. Preheat grill to high.
2. Slice each okra down its length, stopping just short of the end, then transfer to a large bowl. Add the olive oil, salt, and pepper, then toss until evenly coated.
3. Add the sour cream, mayonnaise, chipotle, adobo sauce, lime juice, and a pinch of salt to a blender and process until well combined. Pour the sauce into a small bowl and set aside.
4. When your grill is hot, spread the okra in a single layer over direct heat, or in a perforated grill pan if your grates are too wide. Close the lid and cook for about 2 minutes, then flip the okra over and continue flipping until evenly grilled on all sides, about 5-7 minutes total.
5. Immediately transfer the grilled okra to a serving plate and serve with the chipotle sauce.

HOPPIN' JOHN

Black-eyed peas are a Southern staple, usually prepared with ham or bacon and seasoned the way you like. Adding peas to steamed long-grain white rice makes Hoppin' John, a classic Southern dish.

SERVES 6

1 1-pound ham steak
1 teaspoon salt
½ teaspoon ground black pepper
1 tablespoon vegetable oil
1 large onion, chopped
1 celery rib, diced
4 garlic cloves, minced

6 cups chicken broth
Salt and ground black pepper, to taste
4 cups fresh black-eyed peas
2 cups uncooked long-grain white rice
2 tablespoons unsalted butter
3 cups water

1. Preheat grill to high.
2. Rinse the ham under running water, then pat dry and trim off any excess fat. Season both sides with salt and black pepper.
3. When your grill is hot, use tongs to dip a wad of paper towels in vegetable oil and run them a dozen times across the grates. Grill ham over direct heat until grill marks begin to appear and the ham is cooked through, about 5 minutes on each side. Allow the ham to cool, then roughly chop.
4. Heat vegetable oil in a large Dutch oven over direct heat, then cook onion, celery, and garlic until tender, about 5 minutes. Add broth, salt, black pepper, and peas and bring to a boil. Lower the heat and simmer until peas are tender and creamy, about 45 minutes. Add chopped ham and stir.
5. Add rice, butter, and water to a medium pot on your stovetop and bring to a boil. Reduce heat to medium-low, cover, and let simmer for 15 minutes. Remove pot from heat and allow rice to rest for 5 minutes, then fluff with a fork.
6. Spoon rice onto plates and top with the peas and ham.

LOUISIANA DEEP-FRIED RIBS

Deep-fried ribs is a Louisiana specialty that is starting to show up in restaurants around Chicago. When people tell me they're from the South, I ask them if they've eaten deep-fried ribs. If the answer is no, I know they're not really from the South.

SERVES 8

4 racks baby back ribs
6 cups Coca-Cola
4 cups milk
4 eggs
2 cups all-purpose flour
6 cups ketchup
2 cups dark brown sugar
¾ cup chili powder
½ cup ground black pepper
¼ cup dry mustard
2 tablespoons ground cinnamon

Grill Seasoning:
1 tablespoon cumin
1 tablespoon paprika
1 tablespoon granulated garlic
1 tablespoon granulated onion
1 tablespoon chili powder
1 tablespoon brown sugar
2 tablespoons Kosher salt
2 teaspoons pepper
1 teaspoon cayenne pepper

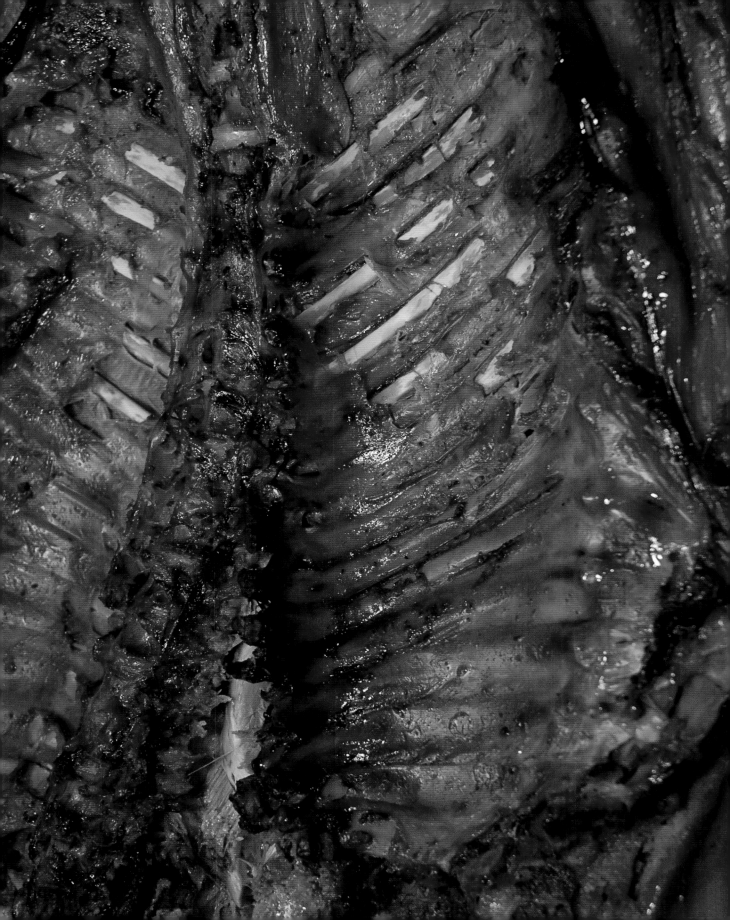

LOUISIANA DEEP-FRIED RIBS
(continued)

1. Place ribs in a large glass or ceramic dish and pour 4 cups of Coca-Cola over them. Tightly cover with plastic wrap and let the ribs marinate overnight in the refrigerator.

2. Preheat grill to medium. Rinse each rack under water, pat dry, and remove the thin membrane on the underside of the ribs, if necessary. Combine grill seasoning ingredients in a bowl and mix to combine.

3. When your grill is hot, stack one rack on top of the other and cook over indirect heat for 30 minutes. Remove ribs and rub each side with grill seasoning, then return them to the grill for another 90 minutes, rotating them every 30 minutes. Remove ribs and cool completely.

4. In a large Dutch oven, heat 1 gallon of peanut oil to 350 degrees. (If you own a deep fryer, follow the manufacturer's instructions.) Depending on your fryer, it might be easier to cut the ribs into individual sections at this point.

5. In a shallow dish, mix milk and eggs. In another dish, mix flour and any remaining grill seasoning. Dip ribs into egg mixture, then dredge through the breading mixture. Shake off the excess, then repeat. Carefully place ribs into the oil in batches and cook for 5 minutes or until golden brown.

6. Pour 2 cups of Coca-Cola into a blender or food processor and add the ketchup, brown sugar, chili powder, black pepper, dry mustard, and cinnamon. Mix until smooth and well blended, then pour into a saucepan and simmer until it thickens, about 20 minutes. Serve alongside ribs.

GRILLED GREEN TOMATOES CAPRESE SALAD

Everyone has heard of fried green tomatoes, but here's a lighter version you can make on your grill. Green tomatoes tend to be more firm and sour than red tomatoes—grilling them and then pairing them with balsamic vinegar and good fresh mozzarella helps bring out a bright flavor.

SERVES 6

5-6 medium green tomatoes, cut into thick slices
½ cup extra-virgin olive oil
¼ cup balsamic vinegar
2 garlic cloves, minced
1 tablespoon brown sugar

1 16-ounce package fresh mozzarella cheese, cut into thick slices
½ cup fresh basil, thinly sliced
Kosher salt and ground black pepper, to taste

1. Place tomatoes in a large resealable bag, then add olive oil, balsamic vinegar, garlic, and brown sugar. Make sure the slices are evenly coated, then seal the bag and refrigerate for at least 1 hour.
2. Preheat grill to medium-high.
3. When your grill is hot, remove tomatoes from marinade and cook, with the lid closed, until grill marks begin to appear, about 3-4 minutes on each side.
4. Alternate slices of tomatoes and mozzarella on a large platter, then drizzle with reserved marinade and sprinkle with basil. Season with salt and black pepper to taste.

BEEF

BEEF RIBS

Beef ribs are more popular in Texas than they are in my home state of Georgia, but there's something to be said for this rich and succulent cut of beef. Plus, they're actually fairly easy to prepare if you give yourself enough time. Ask your butcher for plate ribs, which has more meat and fat than back ribs.

SERVES 2–4

1 rack of plate ribs, usually sold in 3-bone portions, about 3-5 pounds
1 tablespoon hot sauce
2 tablespoons sweet paprika
1 tablespoon chili powder
1 tablespoon ground cumin
1 tablespoon dark brown sugar

1 tablespoon Kosher salt
½ tablespoon dried oregano
½ tablespoon sugar
1 tablespoon ground black pepper
1 teaspoon cayenne pepper
1 cup apple juice

1. Soak 3-4 cups of wood chunks in cold water for about an hour, then drain. Pour the apple juice into a clean spray bottle.
2. Preheat grill to medium-low, about 275 degrees.
3. Slather the ribs with hot sauce, which builds flavor and also helps the rub stick to the meat. Add the paprika, chili powder, cumin, brown sugar, salt, oregano, sugar, black pepper, and cayenne pepper to a small bowl and mix to combine. Liberally rub the mixture into all sides of the ribs.
4. Transfer the wood chips to a smoker box or vented foil pouch and heat until they begin to smoke. Cook the ribs, bone side down, on the cooler side of the grill until they develop a nice bark, about 4-5 hours. Spray the ribs occasionally with apple juice to keep the bark from getting too dark. Repeat the process until the meat is tender but not falling off the bone, or until the internal temperature reaches 205 degrees, about 2-3 more hours. Remove the ribs and allow to rest for 15 minutes.

BEEF TENDERLOIN WITH ARUGULA AND SHAVED PARMESAN

This is a great dish for a date night or any special occasion—it results in an impressive looking plate with a minimum amount of effort. I like the buttery flavor of beef tenderloin with the peppery taste of the arugula, but you can use any thick cut of steak you like.

SERVES 2

2 6-ounce beef tenderloins
Kosher salt and ground black pepper, to
    taste

4 cups arugula
6 tablespoons extra virgin olive oil
3 ounces Parmesan cheese

1. Bring the steaks to room temperature, then pat them dry and generously season all sides with salt and black pepper.
2. Preheat grill to high.
3. When your grill is hot, use tongs to dip a wad of paper towels in vegetable oil and run them a dozen times across the grates. Grill the steaks over direct heat, with the lid closed, for 3 minutes, then rotate them 90 degrees and cook for 3 more minutes. Flip the steaks over and repeat the process. After a total of 12 minutes, transfer the steaks to a foil-lined plate and keep them covered for 5 minutes.
4. Divide the arugula evenly between two plates and drizzle each with half of the olive oil. Place one steak in the middle of each plate, as well as any of the juices collected from the foil. Use a vegetable peeler to shave half of the cheese over each plate.

COLD-SMOKED NEW YORK STRIP STEAKS

Smoking a steak before grilling it adds a great flavor usually reserved for foods like brisket or pork. Placing the steaks on a wire rack over ice protects them from the heat of the grill and allows the smoke to penetrate them on all four sides.

SERVES 4

4 New York strip steaks, about 1½- inch thick	Kosher salt and ground black pepper, to taste

1. Soak 3-4 cups of wood chunks in cold water for about an hour, then drain.
2. Bring the steaks to room temperature, then pat them dry and generously season all sides with salt and black pepper. Fill a standard sheet pan with ice cubes, then place a wire rack over the sheet and place the steaks on top.
3. Preheat grill to medium-high.
4. Place the wood chips in a smoker box or vented foil pouch and heat until they begin to smoke. Place the sheet pan with the steaks on the cool side of the grill, as far away from the heat as possible, and close the lid for 3-5 minutes. Remove the steaks, and increase the heat to high.
5. When your grill is hot, use tongs to dip a wad of paper towels in vegetable oil and run them a dozen times across the grates. Grill the steaks over direct heat, with the lid closed, for 2-3 minutes, then rotate them 90 degrees and cook for 2-3 more minutes. Flip the steaks over and repeat the process. Transfer the cooked steaks to a foil-lined plate and keep them covered for 5 minutes.

GRILLED SMOKY MEATLOAF

To me, there are few comfort foods better on this earth than meatloaf. This recipe features some traditional Southern flavors, and grilling the meatloaf in two different ways creates a delicious and smoky crust.

SERVES 6

1 tablespoon butter

3 celery ribs, diced

1 medium onion, diced

1 pound lean ground beef

1 pound ground pork

1 tablespoon Worcestershire sauce

½ cup Italian-seasoned breadcrumbs

⅓ cup ketchup

2 teaspoons Creole seasoning

1 teaspoon Greek seasoning

1 teaspoon garlic powder

2 large eggs, lightly beaten

Salt and ground black pepper, to taste

1 cup ketchup

¼ cup packed brown sugar

2½ tablespoons cider vinegar

½ teaspoon hot sauce

1. Preheat grill to medium-high. Place a disposable foil drip pan under the grates on the indirect-heat side of the grill.
2. Soak 3-4 cups of wood chunks in cold water and then drain.
3. Melt butter in a nonstick skillet over medium heat on your stovetop, then add celery and onion and sauté until tender, about 5-7 minutes.
4. Transfer mixture to a large bowl, then add ground beef, ground pork, Worcestershire sauce, breadcrumbs, ketchup, seasonings, garlic powder, eggs, and salt and black pepper. Mix to combine, then form into a 9 x 5-inch loaf on a piece of aluminum foil.
5. Place the wood chips in a smoker box or vented foil pouch and heat until they begin to smoke. Carefully place the meatloaf, with foil, over the drip pan on the cooler side of the grill—that way, the fat will drain away from the meatloaf and give you a nicer crust. Close the lid and allow to cook for about 45 minutes.
6. Whisk ketchup, brown sugar, cider vinegar, and hot sauce in a saucepan and heat until the sauce has thickened and the sugar is fully dissolved, about 5 minutes.
7. After 45 minutes, glaze the meatloaf, then close the lid for another 10 minutes. Repeat the process until the meatloaf's internal temperature reaches 160 degrees. Remove the meatloaf and allow to rest for 5 minutes.
8. Cut the meatloaf into thick slices and grill over direct heat until grill marks begin to appear, about 3-4 minutes. Baste with the remaining glaze and serve.

MUSTARD-CRUSTED STEAK KEBABS

Most people marinate their steak kebabs in soy or teriyaki sauce, but down South, we like to use mustard. This garlic-mustard marinade forms a crust on your kebabs, leaving you with steak that has a crispy exterior and a juicy center.

SERVES 6

¼ cup whole grain mustard
2 tablespoons Dijon mustard
4 garlic cloves, finely chopped
2 tablespoons white wine vinegar
1 tablespoon soy sauce
1 tablespoon honey
1 tablespoon fresh rosemary leaves, finely chopped

2 pounds beef tenderloin, sliced into 1-inch pieces
¼ teaspoon Kosher salt
¼ teaspoon ground black pepper
1 red bell pepper, sliced into 1-inch pieces
1 yellow bell pepper, sliced into 1-inch pieces
1 red onion, sliced into 1-inch pieces

1. Soak wooden skewers in water for at least 30 minutes, then drain.
2. Add mustards, garlic, vinegar, soy sauce, honey, and rosemary to a bowl, then whisk to combine. Pat beef dry, then season all sides with salt and black pepper. Divide four pieces of beef, slices of bell peppers, and onion among six skewers. Place the assembled skewers in a baking dish, pour half of the marinade over the meat, and coat thoroughly.
3. Preheat grill to high.
4. When your grill is hot, use tongs to dip a wad of paper towels in vegetable oil and run them a dozen times across the grates. Grill the skewers, turning once and basting with remaining marinade, until grill marks begin to appear and the steak is cooked through, about 5-8 minutes.

RED-WINE-MARINATED RIBEYE

If you have a good ribeye steak, there's very little you need to do before grilling it other than season it with salt and pepper. But I like to use this red-wine marinade—it adds a slight acidity to the meat and helps break down the fat for a tender, juicy steak.

SERVES 2

½ cup dry red wine
¼ cup soy sauce
2 tablespoons honey
¼ cup brown sugar
2 tablespoons Worcestershire sauce
1 tablespoon fresh rosemary leaves, chopped

1 tablespoon thyme, chopped
3 garlic cloves, minced
2 ribeye steaks
2 teaspoons Kosher salt
1 teaspoon ground black pepper

1. In a medium bowl, whisk together the wine, soy sauce, honey, brown sugar, Worcestershire sauce, rosemary, thyme, and garlic. Place the steaks in a large resealable bag, then pour in the marinade and make sure the meat is well covered. Refrigerate for at least 6 hours.
2. Preheat grill to high.
3. Remove the steaks from the marinade and pat them dry, then season generously with salt and black pepper.
4. When your grill is hot, use tongs to dip a wad of paper towels in vegetable oil and run them a dozen times across the grates. Grill the steaks over direct heat, with the lid closed, until grill marks begin to appear, about 4 minutes per side.

HERB-CRUSTED RIB ROAST

When you're cooking for a large group, a big cut of meat can be the best way to go. Keep in mind that a rib roast is a dense piece of beef, so don't t be shy with the seasoning.

SERVES 12

1 boneless rib roast, about 5-6 pounds

3 teaspoons Kosher salt

2 teaspoons ground black pepper

½ cup Dijon mustard

½ cup shallots, finely chopped

6 garlic cloves, minced

3 teaspoons fresh thyme, finely chopped

2 pounds beef bones

1½ cups low-sodium beef broth

1. Trim the rib roast of any excess fat, then sprinkle salt and pepper evenly on all sides. Add the mustard, shallots, garlic, and thyme in another small bowl and mix to combine. Set aside ¼ cup of the mixture, then spread the rest over all sides of the roast. Let the roast sit at room temperature for at least an hour.
2. Preheat grill to medium.
3. Place one large disposable foil pan inside of the other, then put the bones in the pan and carefully set the roast on top with the fat side facing up. When you grill reaches about 350 degrees, arrange the pan on the indirect side of the grill with the roast's thicker end facing the heat, then close the lid. Rotate the roast after 1 hour, then continue cooking until the internal temperature reaches 125 degrees, about 2 hours total. Remove the roast, cover with aluminum foil, and allow to rest for 20-30 minutes.
4. Remove and discard the bones, as well as the clear fat, from the pan, then return it to the grill over direct heat. When the remaining brown bits begin to crackle, add the beef broth and the reserved mustard mixture. Continue cooking until the mixture is hot—make sure to scrape any brown bits off the bottom. Remove the pan and season the sauce with salt and black pepper.
5. Cut the roast into ½-inch slices and serve with the au jus.

EASY GRILLED BRISKET

Brisket might be the grandaddy of all BBQ meats and is one of the most flavorful cuts you'll ever enjoy. Most people think it's too hard to cook right, but if you have the time and find the right piece of meat, you won't regret it.

SERVES 10

1 5-6 pound brisket
¼ cup brown sugar
¼ cup smoked paprika

2 tablespoons sea salt
1 tablespoon ground black pepper
1 tablespoon ground white pepper

1. If your supermarket only has briskets on the smaller side, you might have to find a butcher shop or specialty grocery store—trust me, you don't want to spend hours cooking a 2-3 pound brisket.

2. Once you get your brisket home, pat it dry with paper towels. Combine the brown sugar, paprika, salt, and peppers in a small bowl, then rub the mixture on all sides of the meat. Wrap the brisket in aluminum foil and set aside for at least an hour. At the same time, soak 3-4 cups of wood chunks in cold water, then drain.

3. Remove brisket from fridge and allow to come to room temperature.

4. Preheat grill to medium-low. Place the wood chips in a smoker box or vented foil pouch and heat until they begin to smoke. Place a disposable foil roasting pan under the grate on the indirect side of the grill.

5. When your grill is about 220-250 degrees, place brisket over the foil pan on the indirect side of the grill. Add water to a second foil pan and place it next to the brisket—this will help keep the meat moist and also helps you make sure your grill is at the right temperature (if the water is boiling, the grill is too hot). Grill the brisket for about 1 hour per pound, or until the internal temperature measures at least 200 degrees.

6. Allow brisket to rest for an hour, then cut across the grain and serve.

PORK

GRILLED LEMON-BASIL PORK CHOPS

Down South, everyone fries their pork chops, but here's a healthier version I've grown to love over the years. Make sure your pork chops are thick enough to stand up to the high heat.

SERVES 4

---

2 tablespoons fresh lemon juice
2 tablespoons olive oil
3 garlic cloves, minced
⅛ teaspoon dried basil

4 thick-cut boneless pork loin chops
⅛ teaspoon ground black pepper
¾ tablespoon salt

---

1. Add the lemon juice, olive oil, garlic, and basil to a medium bowl, then whisk until blended.
2. Place the pork chops in a large resealable bag, then pour in the marinade and make sure the chops are well covered. Refrigerate for several hours or overnight.
3. Preheat grill to high.
4. Remove the chops from the marinade and pat dry, then season with salt and black pepper. Pour the remaining marinade in a sauce pan and bring to a boil, then set aside to cool.
5. When your grill is hot, use tongs to dip a wad of paper towels in vegetable oil and run them a dozen times across the grates. Cook pork chops over direct heat, basting frequently with the cooled marinade, until the internal temperature reaches 145 degrees, about 5-7 minutes per side.

PORK GYROS WITH TZATZIKI SAUCE

Gyros can be found on almost any corner in Chicago—the meat is roasted on a vertical spit, usually in front of an electric broiler, then served on a pita with vegetables and a yogurt-based sauce. Here's a version you can make in your backyard using pork tenderloin, along with a classic recipe for tzatziki.

SERVES 4

¼ cup olive oil
¼ cup red wine
4 garlic cloves, chopped
1 tablespoon fresh oregano, chopped
2 pounds pork tenderloin
Salt and ground black pepper, to taste
4 pitas
½ red onion, thinly sliced
1 cup lettuce, shredded
1 plum tomato, thinly sliced

Tzatziki Sauce
1 cucumber, peeled and diced
1 tablespoon salt
1 garlic clove, minced
3 tablespoons lemon juice
1 tablespoon fresh dill
Salt and ground black pepper, to taste
3 cups Greek yogurt

PORK GYROS WITH TZATZIKI SAUCE (continued)

1. To prepare the tzatziki sauce, place cucumber in a colander and sprinkle with salt to draw out any extra water. Cover with a plate and set aside for 30 minutes, then drain well and pat dry. Add cucumbers, garlic, lemon juice, dill, and black pepper to a blender or food processor. When ingredients are well blended, add them to the yogurt in a large bowl and stir to combine. Add salt if needed, then refrigerate for at least 2 hours.

2. Add the olive oil, wine, garlic, and oregano to a baking dish and whisk to combine. Add the pork tenderloin and turn to coat in the marinade, then refrigerate for at least 2 hours.

3. Preheat grill to high.

4. When your grill is hot, use tongs to dip a wad of paper towels in vegetable oil and run them a dozen times across the grates. Remove the pork from the baking dish and pat dry, then season with salt and black pepper. Grill the pork until golden brown on all sides and the internal temperature reaches 150 degrees, about 16-20 minutes. Cover the pork with foil and allow to rest for 5 minutes, then cut into thin slices.

5. Grill each pita for a few seconds on each side until they begin to brown. Fill each pita with pork, lettuce, onion, tomato, and tzatziki sauce.

SMOKED PORK SHOULDER WITH SPICY TOMATOES

Pork shoulder is prepared many ways, but here's a recipe for feeding a crowd that pairs the meat with a mixture of ripe tomatoes and spices you may have in your cupboard.

SERVES 6–8

1 tablespoon Kosher salt
1½ teaspoons ground black pepper
1 teaspoon garlic powder
1 teaspoon paprika
½ teaspoon ground cayenne pepper
1 boneless pork shoulder roast (3-4 pounds)
1½ pounds ripe tomatoes

1 tablespoon vegetable oil
1 yellow onion, finely chopped
½ teaspoon cumin seed
½ teaspoon ground coriander
¾ cup red wine vinegar
⅛ cup granulated sugar
¼ cup golden raisins

1. Mix the salt, black pepper, garlic powder, paprika, and cayenne pepper in a small bowl. Set aside 1 teaspoon, then spread the rest over all sides of the roast. Wrap the roast in plastic wrap and refrigerate overnight.

2. Preheat grill to low.

3. Allow the pork to stand at room temperature for 30 minutes before grilling. At the same time, soak 3-4 cups of wood chunks in cold water and then drain.

4. Place the wood chips in a smoker box or vented foil pouch and heat until they begin to smoke, then cook the tomatoes over direct heat until soft, about 30 minutes, turning occasionally. Remove from the grill and allow to cool, then peel, core, and roughly chop.

5. Cook the roast over the indirect side of the grill, with the lid closed, until the meat is tender but not falling apart, about 3-4 hours. When the internal temperature has reached 185 degrees, remove the meat from the grill, cover it with aluminum foil, and allow to rest.

6. Heat the oil in a saucepan over medium heat, then add the onion, cumin seed, coriander, and the reserved rub and cook until the onion is tender, about 8 minutes. Add the tomatoes, vinegar, sugar, and raisins to the pan and cook until thickened, about 25 minutes. Season with salt and black pepper.

7. Cut the roast into ½-inch slices and serve with the spicy tomato mixture.

PULLED PORK SANDWICHES

When you have a big backyard full of people to feed, it's tough to beat pulled pork that's been smoked until it's fork tender. Make sure you leave yourself plenty of time for this one—it's not hard to make but does take some patience. Serve this classic favorite topped with cole slaw and call it Southern style. You can also find a version of this sandwich at the Big Hurt Brewhouse.

SERVES 12

4 tablespoons sweet paprika

2 tablespoons chili powder

2 tablespoons ground cumin

2 tablespoons dark brown sugar

2 tablespoons salt

1 tablespoon dried oregano

1 tablespoon sugar

2 tablespoons ground black pepper

2 teaspoons cayenne pepper

1 bone-in pork roast, preferably Boston butt (6-8 pounds)

Easy Barbecue Sauce

2 tablespoons vegetable oil

1 onion, finely chopped

3 garlic cloves, minced

1½ cups ketchup

½ cup cider vinegar

¼ cup Worcestershire sauce

⅓ cup sugar

1 tablespoon chili powder

½ teaspoon cayenne pepper

1. Add paprika, chili powder, cumin, brown sugar, salt, oregano, sugar, black pepper, and cayenne pepper to a small bowl and mix to combine. Rub the mixture into the pork roast, then wrap meat tightly with two layers of plastic wrap and refrigerate for at least 3 hours.

2. About 1 hour prior to cooking, unwrap the roast and let it come to room temperature. At the same time, soak 3-4 cups of wood chunks in cold water and then drain.

3. Heat the vegetable oil in a saucepan over medium heat, then cook the onion and garlic for about 5 minutes. Add the ketchup, vinegar, Worcestershire sauce, sugar, chili powder, and cayenne pepper, then reduce the heat and simmer until the sauce has thickened, about 20 minutes. Transfer to a bowl and set aside.

4. Preheat grill to high. Place the wood chips in a smoker box or vented foil pouch and heat until they begin to smoke. Turn the heat down to medium. When your grill is about 250 degrees, place the pork on the grill and cook until it is fork-tender and the internal temperature reaches 165 degrees, about 5-6 hours. Rotate the meat every 45 minutes.

5. Transfer the pork to a rimmed baking sheet. When cool enough to handle, use two large forks to shred the meat into bite-size pieces. Mound the meat onto a platter and toss with 1 cup of the barbecue sauce. Serve the remaining sauce with the buns of your choice.

SPICY TACOS AL PASTOR

Tacos al pastor are a Mexican classic—strips of pork that are crispy on the outside but tender on the inside—but roasting marinated pork on a rotisserie for hours and then shaving it into tortillas is a little impractical at home. The secret to this simple recipe is using boneless pork ribs, which eliminates much of the prep work and speeds up the cooking time. You can find dried guajillo chiles in any Mexican grocery story and most supermarkets.

SERVES 6

10 dried guajillo chiles
1¼ pounds plum tomatoes
1½ cups water
8 garlic cloves
4 bay leaves
2 teaspoons salt
¾ teaspoon sugar

½ teaspoon cumin
½ teaspoon ground black pepper
3 pounds boneless pork ribs
1 small onion, halved
½ cup cilantro, roughly chopped
½ cup queso fresco
12 corn or flour tortillas

SPICY TACOS AL PASTOR
(continued)

1. Heat a large Dutch oven over medium heat on your stovetop. Roast the chiles 5 at a time in the dry pot until they begin to soften and release their fragrance, about 3-4 minutes. Set aside.

2. Core the tomatoes and then cut them into halves. Add the tomatoes, water, garlic, bay leaves, salt, sugar, cumin, and black pepper, and cook the mixture over medium-high heat. Tear off the stems of the chiles and submerge them in the liquid, including seeds. Cook for about 20 minutes.

3. Transfer the cooked liquid into a blender and blend until smooth. Pour the blended mixture through a mesh strainer back into the pot and turn the heat down to medium-low. Submerge the pork ribs into the sauce and allow to cook, mostly covered, until the pork is tender but not falling apart, about 90 minutes.

4. Preheat grill to high. When your grill is hot, use tongs to dip a wad of paper towels in vegetable oil and run them a dozen times across the grates. Grill the pork until it begins to char, about 3-5 minutes per side, basting each side with some of the sauce. Cut the pork into bite-size strips and toss with the remaining sauce.

5. Grill the onions until they begin to blacken and soften, then remove and slice. Serve along with the cilantro, queso fresco, and tortillas.

SPICY SOUTHWESTERN HAM STEAK

A ham steak makes a perfect weekday meal in the summer, when you want to fire up the grill and eat outside but don't have time to do a lot of preparation. The brown sugar in this rub gives the ham a nice crusty exterior.

SERVES 6–8

1 tablespoon chile powder
2 teaspoons dried oregano
2 teaspoons brown sugar
½ teaspoon cayenne pepper

¼ teaspoon ground black pepper
1 tablespoon unsalted butter, melted
1 center-cut smoked ham steak, about 2-3 pounds and 1-2 inches thick

1. Preheat grill to medium-high.
2. Add the chile powder, oregano, brown sugar, cayenne pepper, and black pepper in a small bowl, then mix to combine. Brush both sides of the ham steak with butter—this helps the rub stick better to the meat. Season both sides evenly with the spice mixture, pressing it into the meat.
3. When your grill is hot, use tongs to dip a wad of paper towels in vegetable oil and run them a dozen times across the grates. Grill the ham steak over direct heat, with the lid closed, until it is nicely browned on both sides, about 12-15 minutes total. Remove from the grill and serve warm.

GRILLED PORK TENDERLOIN SANDWICH WITH CAROLINA MUSTARD SAUCE

Pork tenderloins are another great option when you're short on time but are looking for something to grill. Mustard sauce is a classic in South Carolina, and will keep in your refrigerator for a couple of weeks.

SERVES 6

¾ cup yellow mustard
½ cup honey
¼ cup apple cider vinegar
2 tablespoons ketchup
1 tablespoon brown sugar
2 teaspoons Worcestershire sauce
1 teaspoon hot sauce
1 teaspoon garlic powder

1 teaspoon salt
1 teaspoon dry mustard
½ teaspoon coarsely ground black pepper
2 pork tenderloins, ¾ pound each
1 tablespoon lime juice
1 avocado, mashed
Salt and ground black pepper, to taste
1 cup shredded lettuce

1. Add the mustard, honey, vinegar, ketchup, brown sugar, Worcestershire sauce, and hot sauce to a small bowl and mix to combine. Store in a covered container overnight in your refrigerator to allow the flavors to meld.
2. Preheat grill to medium-high.
3. Mix the garlic powder, salt, dry mustard, and black pepper in a small bowl, and spread evenly over the tenderloins.
4. When your grill is hot, use tongs to dip a wad of paper towels in vegetable oil and run them a dozen times across the grates. Grill the tenderloins over direct heat, with the lid closed, until the internal temperature reaches 155 degrees, about 10-12 minutes per side. Remove from grill and allow to rest for 10 minutes.
5. Mix lime juice into mashed avocado and season with salt and pepper, then spread over one side of each sandwich roll. Slice the tenderloins and add to the rolls with shredded lettuce and drizzling of mustard sauce.

xfinity
MORE OF THE SOX WITH XFINITY ON DEMAND
HALL-OF-FAMER
FRANK THOMAS

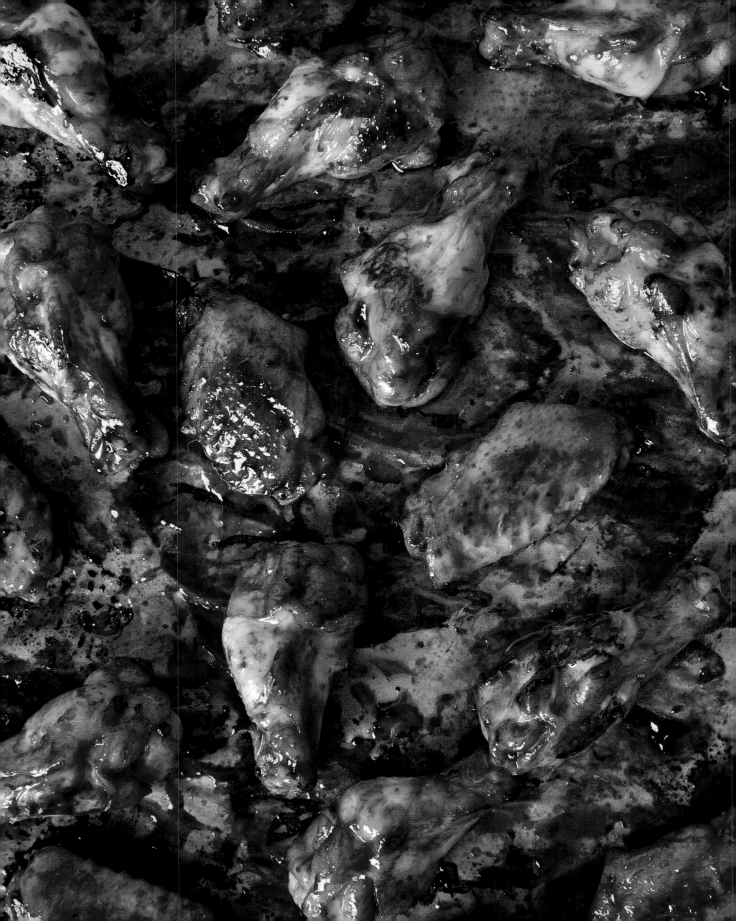

POULTRY

BIG HURT'S BEER CAN CHICKEN

Beer can chicken is a summertime staple around our backyard. Cooked over a can of your favorite beer, the chicken will stay moist on the inside while getting nice and crispy on the outside. The roasting pan catches all of the drippings, making this an easy and worry-free meal.

SERVES 4

2 tablespoons Kosher salt
1½ tablespoons brown sugar
1 tablespoon sweet paprika

½ tablespoon cayenne pepper
1 12-ounce can beer
1 chicken, about 4 pounds

1. Combine salt, brown sugar, paprika, and cayenne pepper in a bowl and mix. Liberally rub mixture all over the chicken and set aside.

2. Enjoy (or pour out) half of your beer, leaving half the can full.

3. Preheat grill to high. Place a disposable foil roasting pan over the cool side of the grill and fill with about ½ inch water.

4. When your grill is hot, place cavity of chicken, legs pointing down, over open can so that it supports chicken upright. Place can, with chicken, on grill above the roasting pan to catch the drippings. Close lid and grill chicken for 25-30 minutes, then rotate the pan so that the other side of the chicken is facing direct heat. Cook another 20-30 minutes, or until an instant-read thermometer inserted into the thickest part of thigh registers 165 degrees. Let chicken rest 10 minutes before carving.

DEVIL'S CHICKEN THIGHS

The inspiration behind this dish is the classic *fra diavolo* sauce, so popular in Italian kitchens. The spicy marinade is a great pairing with the dark meat of chicken thighs, but you can also use chicken breasts or peeled and cleaned shrimp.

SERVES 6

1 red pepper, diced
2 jalapeño peppers, cleaned and diced
6 garlic cloves, peeled
½ cup extra virgin olive oil
2 tablespoons fresh thyme leaves
2 tablespoons red chili flakes

2 tablespoons smoked paprika
1 tablespoon ground black pepper
Zest and juice of two oranges (about ⅔ cup)
12 bone-in, skin-on chicken thighs

1. Place the red pepper, jalapeño peppers, garlic, and olive oil in your blender or food processor and blend until smooth. Transfer to a bowl and add thyme, red chili flakes, paprika, black pepper, and the orange zest and juice, then whisk until blended.

2. Place the chicken thighs in a large resealable bag, then pour in the marinade and make sure the chicken is well covered. Refrigerate for several hours or overnight.

3. Preheat grill to medium-high. When your grill is hot, use tongs to dip a wad of paper towels in vegetable oil and run them a dozen times across the grates. Cook chicken thighs over direct heat until the internal temperature reaches 165 degrees, about 5 minutes per side.

GRILLED TURKEY LEGS

When most people think about turkey legs, they're either imagining a Thanksgiving dinner or walking around with one at a state fair. But grilling turkey legs is a lot easier than you think, and brining them first will make sure they turn out crispy on the outside and juicy on the inside.

SERVES 6

½ onion, sliced
4 garlic cloves, smashed
3 tablespoons sugar
4 tablespoons Kosher salt
36 ounces beer
1 bay leaf
1 teaspoon black peppercorns
4 cups cold water or ice

6 turkey legs
1 teaspoon ground mustard
2 tablespoons granulated garlic
1 tablespoon granulated onion
3 tablespoons smoked paprika
1 tablespoon light brown sugar
1 teaspoon ground black pepper

---

1. Combine onion, garlic, sugar, 3 tablespoons of salt, beer, bay leaf, and peppercorns in a large pot and bring to a simmer. After the sugar and salt is fully dissolved, add water or ice and allow to cool. Add turkey legs to brine and refrigerate overnight.

2. Preheat grill to medium.

3. Combine mustard, garlic, onion, paprika, brown sugar, 1 tablespoon of salt, and black pepper in a small bowl. Remove turkey legs from brine and pat dry. Sprinkle with dry mixture.

4. Place the turkey legs on the grill over direct heat until brown on all sides, about 5-8 minutes.

5. Move the legs to the cooler part of the grill and close the lid. Continue cooking until just cooked through or until the internal temperature reaches 180 degrees, about 45-60 minutes. Remove from the grill and let rest 10 minutes before serving.

GRILLED CHICKEN AND PEACHES SALAD

There's something about grilled peaches that just feels like summer, and adding them to a spinach and chicken salad makes a delicious weekday meal.

SERVES 4–6

¼ cup extra virgin olive oil
1 tablespoon balsamic vinegar
1 shallot, minced
1 teaspoon Dijon mustard
½ teaspoon salt

4 peaches, halved and pitted
4 skinless, boneless chicken breasts
Salt and ground black pepper, to taste
8 cups baby spinach

1. Add olive oil, balsamic vinegar, shallot, Dijon mustard, and salt to a small bowl and whisk until well combined.
2. Preheat grill to medium-high. When your grill is hot, use tongs to dip a wad of paper towels in vegetable oil and run them a dozen times across the grates.
3. Brush the cut side of peaches with oil, then cook over direct heat until grill marks begin to appear, about 4 minutes. Remove from grill and set aside.
4. Season chicken breasts with salt and black pepper, then grill until the internal temperature reaches 165 degrees, about 4-5 minutes per side.
5. Slice chicken into thin pieces and cut peaches into ½-inch cubes.
6. Toss spinach and dressing together in a large bowl until the leaves are evenly coated. Divide salad among plates and top with chicken and peaches.

BBQ CHICKEN SANDWICH WITH BACON PASTE

Making a paste out of raw bacon might seem a little strange, but trust me, it adds some delicious flavor to ordinary chicken breasts.

SERVES 4

¾ cup ketchup
2 tablespoons light brown sugar
1 tablespoon white wine vinegar
1 tablespoon Worcestershire sauce
¼ teaspoon cayenne pepper
2 teaspoons Kosher salt
1 teaspoon ground black pepper
½ teaspoon garlic powder

½ teaspoon onion powder
2 tablespoons paprika
3 tablespoons dark brown sugar
4 slices raw bacon, cut into small pieces
4 skinless, boneless chicken breasts
1 cup lettuce, shredded
½ tomato, sliced

1. Add ketchup, light brown sugar, vinegar, Worcestershire sauce, and cayenne pepper to a small saucepan and cook over medium heat on your stovetop, stirring occasionally, until the sauce has thickened, about 7 minutes.

2. Combine salt, black pepper, garlic powder, onion powder, paprika, dark brown sugar, and bacon to your food processor and pulse until completely smooth, about 45-60 seconds. Rub the bacon mixture evenly over the chicken breasts and refrigerate for 1 hour.

3. Preheat grill to medium-high. When your grill is hot, use tongs to dip a wad of paper towels in vegetable oil and run them a dozen times across the grates. Grill chicken over direct heat for 4 minutes, then baste with sauce and continue cooking for 1 minute. Repeat the process on the other side, then remove chicken from grill once the internal temperature reaches 165 degrees.

4. Place each chicken breast on a hearty bun and top with sauce, lettuce, and tomato.

HONEY SRIRACHA CHICKEN DRUMSTICKS

If you're looking for a new way to prepare chicken drumsticks, try this combination of sweet-and-spicy honey sriracha. Sear these sticky wings in a hot cast-iron pan, then close the lid and let your grill do the rest.

SERVES 6

12 chicken drumsticks
Salt and ground black pepper, to taste
½ cup soy sauce
2 tablespoons balsamic vinegar
2 tablespoons lime juice

½ cup honey
2 tablespoons sriracha
4 garlic cloves, minced
2 teaspoons fresh ginger, grated
Sesame seeds, for garnish

1. Preheat grill to high. Grease the bottom and sides of the cast-iron skillet with vegetable oil, then place on the grill to warm.
2. Pat chicken dry and season generously with salt and black pepper. In a small bowl, combine soy sauce, balsamic vinegar, lime juice, honey, sriracha, minced garlic, and grated ginger.
3. When your pan is hot, brown the drumsticks in the skillet on all sides, brushing with sauce, about 5 minutes. Move the pan to the cooler side of the grill and close the lid. Bake the drumsticks until they are cooked through and the skin is crispy, regularly turning and basting with the remaining sauce, about 20-25 minutes.
4. Sprinkle with sesame seeds before serving.

LEMON-LIME SODA CHICKEN WINGS

You may not have heard of this one, but trust me, it's a winner. This sweet and salty chicken immediately becomes a favorite of everyone who tries it.

SERVES 10

3 cups lemon-lime soda (not diet)

3 cups soy sauce

3 pounds of chicken drummettes and wingettes

⅓ cup olive oil

1 tablespoon Dijon mustard

3 garlic cloves, minced

¼ cup scallions, chopped

1. Add lemon-lime soda, soy sauce, olive oil, mustard, garlic, and scallions to a bowl, then mix to combine. Place the chicken in large resealable bags, then pour in the marinade and make sure the chicken is well covered. Refrigerate for at least 8 hours or overnight.

2. Heat grill to medium. When your grill is hot, use tongs to dip a wad of paper towels in vegetable oil and run them a dozen times across the grates.

3. Grill chicken, basting occasionally with the leftover marinade, until the chicken is cooked through, about 5-6 minutes per side.

SWEET CHILI BACON-WRAPPED CHICKEN TENDERS

These bacon-wrapped chicken skewers are easy to prepare and surprisingly tangy. To add even more spice, sprinkle some red chili flakes into the sweet chili sauce before brushing the chicken.

SERVES 4–6

12 chicken tenders
1 teaspoon salt
1 teaspoon ground black pepper

1 cup sweet chili sauce
6 sprigs fresh rosemary
6 strips of bacon, sliced into halves

1. Soak wooden skewers in water for at least 30 minutes, then drain.
2. Preheat grill to medium.
3. Pat chicken tenders dry, then season both sides with salt and black pepper and brush with sweet chili sauce. Skewer each tender along with a sprig of rosemary, then wrap each with one strip of bacon.
5. When your grill is hot, use tongs to dip a wad of paper towels in vegetable oil and run them a dozen times across the grates.
6. Grill chicken, basting occasionally with the remaining sweet chili sauce, until the chicken is cooked through, about 5 minutes per side.

GRILLED ORGANIC TURKEY BREAST

This recipe comes from my good friend Barry S. Dakake, the executive chef at N9NE Steakhouse at the Palms Casino Resort in Las Vegas, Nevada.

SERVES 10–12

1 organic turkey, about 18-20 pounds, or 2 organic boneless turkey breasts, about 4-5 pounds each
¼ cup extra virgin olive oil
¼ cup fresh herbs (parsley, thyme, chives, rosemary, and tarragon), minced

6 garlic cloves, minced
4 shallots, minced
2 Fresno peppers, minced
Cracked black pepper, to taste
Kosher salt, to taste

1. If you have a whole turkey, use a chef's knife and cleaver to separate the backbone, wings, thighs, and drumsticks from the breasts. (The pieces can be roasted and then used to make turkey stock for future use. It'll last a good long time in your freezer.)

2. Add the olive oil, herbs, garlic, shallots, Fresno peppers, and black pepper to a bowl and mix to combine. Place the turkey breasts in a large resealable bag, then pour in the marinade and make sure the turkey is well covered. Refrigerate for 4-6 hours. At the same time, soak 3-4 cups of cherry wood chunks in cold water, then drain.

3. Preheat grill to medium. Place a disposable foil drip pan under the grates on the indirect side of the grill. Place the wood chips in a smoker box or vented foil pouch and heat until they begin to smoke.

4. Remove the turkey breasts from the marinade, pat dry, and season with salt. When your grill is hot, place turkey over the foil pan on the indirect side of the grill and cook, rotating occasionally, until the internal temperature reaches 165 degrees, about 2-3 hours. Allow the turkey to rest for 15-20 minutes before slicing.

SEAFOOD

BLACKENED SHRIMP TACOS

I love the flavor of blackened shrimp, and serving them in tacos is an easy way to serve a large group. This recipe can be expanded to satisfy any size party.

SERVES 4

1 pound of medium shrimp, peeled and deveined
2 teaspoons paprika
1 teaspoon ground cumin
1 teaspoon garlic powder
½ teaspoon dried oregano
¼ teaspoon dried thyme
¼ teaspoon cayenne pepper

¼ teaspoon salt
1 tablespoon vegetable oil
1 cup fresh or thawed corn kernels
8 tortillas
6 ounces queso fresco
1 ripe avocado, sliced
½ cup fresh cilantro, chopped

1. Combine seasonings in a large resealable plastic bag. Add shrimp to bag, seal, and shake well to coat. Remove shrimp and set aside.
2. Preheat grill to high, then grill shrimp for about 2 minutes per side or until nicely charred.
3. Coat a cast-iron pan with vegetable oil, then place over direct heat. Squeeze corn between several paper towels to remove any excess water, then add corn to pan in a single layer. Cook 5 to 10 minutes, or until golden and crispy, stirring frequently. Move to a bowl and set aside.
4. Heat tortillas over direct heat for about 30 seconds per side, or until the tortillas begin to puff up and turn brown. Keep tortillas warm in a tortilla warmer or between damp paper towels.
5. Allow your guests to make their own tacos using the shrimp, corn, queso fresco, avocado, and cilantro.

GRILLED CATFISH WITH QUINOA AND RADISH SALAD

Catfish is a staple in the South, whether it's grilled, fried, baked, blackened, or otherwise prepared. This is a light and bright summer recipe for catfish that's sure to be a crowd pleaser.

SERVES 4

¾ cup quinoa, rinsed
1 cup water
2 garlic cloves, minced
2 teaspoons olive oil
Salt and ground black pepper, to taste
4 catfish fillets, 4-6 ounces each
2 radishes, thinly sliced
1 medium cucumber, cubed

Lemon Dressing
¼ cup extra virgin olive oil
Zest and juice of one lemon
1 teaspoon Dijon mustard
½ teaspoon honey
Salt and ground black pepper, to taste

1. In a saucepan, combine the quinoa and water. Bring the mixture to a boil, then cover and reduce heat to a simmer. Cook for 15 minutes, then turn off the heat and leave the pot covered for 5 minutes. Use a fork to fluff up the quinoa and mix in the garlic and olive oil. Add salt and pepper to taste.

2. In a small bowl, whisk together the olive oil, lemon juice and zest, mustard, and honey until emulsified. Season with salt and black pepper.

3. Preheat grill to high. When your grill is hot, use tongs to dip a wad of paper towels in vegetable oil and run them a dozen times across the grates.

4. Pat the fillets dry with a paper towel, then sprinkle them with salt and pepper and place them on the grill for 3-4 minutes per side or until they release freely from the grates.

5. Transfer the quinoa, radishes, and cucumbers to a large platter, then top with the catfish fillets. Finish by drizzling the lemon dressing over both the fish and salad.

GRILLED OCTOPUS SKEWERS

Grilled octopus is one of those dishes most people order in restaurants, but it's easier to prepare than you might think. After they've been par boiled, simply toss them on the grill for some serious char flavor. Your grocery store fish counter should be able to provide you with cleaned octopus, but frozen octopus is sometimes even more tender after it's been thawed.

SERVES 6

6 garlic cloves
½ cup red wine vinegar
½ cup extra virgin olive oil
1 cup water

3 rosemary sprigs
3 small octopus, about 1 pound each
2 lemons, quartered

1. Combine garlic, red wine vinegar, olive oil, and water in a large saucepan, then add rosemary and octopus and bring to a boil. Reduce heat to a low simmer and cook for 45-60 minutes or until tender (you'll know the octopus is tender when a sharp knife goes through it very easily). If the braising liquid evaporates too quickly, add a little water and adjust the heat. When finished, allow octopus to cool in the pan.

2. Preheat grill to high. When your grill is hot, use tongs to dip a wad of paper towels in vegetable oil and run them a dozen times across the grates.

3. Cut the cooled octopus into large pieces and grill over direct heat until grill marks begin to appear, about 4-6 minutes on each side. Serve with lemon wedges.

TUNA STEAK WITH WRINKLED POTATOES

Cooking tuna steaks on a hot grill results in a piece of fish that's crusty on the outside but still juicy on the inside. Two important things to keep in mind: always buy the freshest tuna steaks you can find, and never cook them past medium-rare.

SERVES 4

2½ pounds small potatoes, washed
4 tablespoons coarse sea salt
4 tuna steaks, about 8 ounces each

2 tablespoons vegetable oil
Salt and ground black pepper, to taste

---

1. Keep tuna steaks in the refrigerator until you're ready to grill.

2. Place the potatoes in a large pot and add just enough water to cover. Add salt and boil on your stovetop for about 25 minutes, or until the potatoes are tender and the water has evaporated. Leave the dry pot over very low heat, turning the potatoes over until they are wrinkled and covered with a fine layer of salt.

3. Preheat grill to high. When your grill is hot, use tongs to dip a wad of paper towels in vegetable oil and run them a dozen times across the grates. Brush both sides of the tuna steaks with oil and sprinkle with salt and black pepper. Cook over direct heat until they begin to char, about 3-4 minutes. Flip and cook for 1-2 more minutes until medium-rare.

MAPLE-GLAZED SALMON

The sweetness of maple syrup adds a unique flavor to this grilled salmon. Always try and buy the freshest salmon you can find.

SERVES 4

4 tablespoons maple syrup
6 tablespoons balsamic vinegar
2 tablespoons extra virgin olive oil

4 salmon fillets, 6-8 ounces each, with skin
Salt and ground black pepper, to taste
1 lemon, quartered

1. Preheat grill to high.
2. Whisk maple syrup, balsamic vinegar, and olive oil in a bowl, then pour into a resealable plastic bag. Add salmon fillets to bag and let marinate for at least 10 minutes.
3. When your grill is hot, use tongs to dip a wad of paper towels in vegetable oil and run them a dozen times across the grates.
4. Remove the salmon from the bag and sprinkle with salt and black pepper. Place flesh side down over direct heat and close the lid.
5. Flip the salmon onto the skin side after 4 minutes, or when the flesh freely releases from the grates. Grill for 4 minutes on the second side, then serve with lemon wedges.

ABOUT THE AUTHOR

Frank Thomas was born to Charlie Mae and Frank Thomas Sr. in Columbus, Georgia. After a stellar multisport high school career, Frank accepted a football scholarship to Auburn University as a tight end. After playing one season of college football, it became clear that Frank's true calling was on the baseball diamond. He spent the next three years breaking records for the Auburn baseball team, and was selected by the Chicago White Sox with the seventh overall pick in the first round of the 1989 MLB Draft. Frank left Auburn as a three-time All-SEC selection, a consensus All-American, and the school's all-time leader in home runs, RBIs, total bases, extra base hits, slugging percentage, and on-base percentage.

Frank made his major league debut in 1990. Over the next two decades, Frank, also known as "The Big Hurt," solidified his place as one of the all-time greats, playing 19 seasons (16 with Chicago, who retired his No. 35 in 2010), earning a trip to five All-Star games, and winning two American League MVP awards and four Silver Sluggers. Frank was also a member of the 2005 World Series champion Chicago White Sox. A career .301 hitter with an elite .419 on-base percentage, he amassed 521 home runs, 1,704 RBIs, 2,468 hits, and 1,667 walks (10th most all-time), and earned first-ballot induction into the National Baseball Hall of Fame in 2014.

Off the field, Frank is married to his loving wife, Megan, with whom he has five children. Following his playing career, Frank spent three years in the booth for Comcast SportsNet's presentation of White Sox games, before joining FOX/FOX Sports 1 in 2014. Frank is also a partner in a number of different businesses, including his self-titled beverage line Big Hurt Beer and the Big Hurt Brewhouse, a bar/restaurant in Berwyn, Illinois.